SmileRise

SmileRise

A very short Poem

Bachar Samawi

www.SmileRisePoem.com

Bachar Samawi Innovations, LLC
West Dover, Vermont

Copyright © 2021 by Bachar Samawi
Prologue Copyright © 2021 by Bachar Samawi
SmileRise poem Copyright © 2021 by Bachar Samawi

Book design by Bachar Samawi Innovations, LLC. ("BSI")
Jacket design by Bachar Samawi Innovations, LLC
SmileRise poem end-of-verse/end-of-poem/page-corners art by Cliparts Zone
Cover image modified rendering /redrawing by BSI of clipart by Cliparts Zone (https://cliparts.zone) "Cliparts Zone mission is to create and curate the best cliparts online and offer it to users for free..."

Bachar Samawi Innovations, LLC supports the value of copyright, free speech and free expression. Copyright fosters a creative environment that encourages originality, enabling poets, writers and artists to contribute to a vibrant and diverse culture through books, music and other creative productions. You have our gratitude for only buying an authorized edition of this book and for supporting the author's rights. Reproducing, scanning, uploading, distributing any part of this book without written permission is prohibited and is a theft of the author's intellectual property. You may seek written permission to use materials from this book by submitting such request to:
customer_service@BacharSamawiInnovations.com

Published by:
Books & Publishing Division
Bachar Samawi Innovations, LLC.
P. O. Box 842
West Dover, VT 05356

www.BacharSamawiInnovations.com   www.SmileRisePoem.com

Library of Congress Control Number: 2021911518

ISBN 9780578930350

First Edition
June 2021

To my best friend Lilian...

Whose captivating smile was imprinted on my soul at fourteen...

Whose invigorating laughter has resonated in my ears across the Caribbean, Atlantic and Mediterranean...

Whose unwavering loyalty is only surpassed by her goodness...

Contents

Prologue 1
    Laura's smile 2
    Emma's smile 3
    Manchester brunette smile 4
    Collective smile 8
    Heather's smile 9
    Andry's smile 11
SmileRise Poem: Line-by-Line 17
SmileRise Poem: Verse-by-Verse 35
Thanks 41
Index 46

Prologue

Life is a collection of smiles threaded by time.

When the winds of circumstance howl and then subside, it is inevitable that the thread linking those smiles gets tangled into knots of varying complexity.

By taking strength from those smiles, and by practicing patience, diligence, hard work, and, most important, integrity and goodness, we can ultimately unravel even the most tangled threads we may encounter.

This is my philosophy on life. It is a choice. It is my choice.

For more than a year, I've been at a loss. The unavailability of smiles has made it exceedingly difficult to stay true to my philosophy. Nevertheless, the everlasting impressions various smiles made on me over the years carried me through the worst of it.

This scarcity of smiles is directly related to the challenges of the 2020–21 era. Fortunately, these circumstances and their logistics seem to be temporary—certainly not short-lived, but temporary. I cannot but wonder how others among us manage: those who may have a disability that poses a barrier to the sight of or emotion in a smile, those who may live in places where a lack of smiles is not so temporary.

"SmileRise" is a poem that captures what some of those most extraordinary smiles have meant to me. It reflects on how their absence affects me now and what their return (an eventual SmileRise) will mean for the future. To my surprise, this short poem, as personal as it is, seems to have evoked familiar feelings for many people.

I am thankful for the unforgettable smiles that have sustained me. I will list but a few in this prologue, and am looking forward to sharing others in future editions of this book.

Laura's smile

Between 2013 and 2019, while my daughters attended Smith College, I would often take road trips from my home in Vermont to visit them in Northampton, Massachusetts.

Along the way, on MA-2 and the Mohawk Trail, lies Shelburne Falls Coffee Roasters. An aficionado of cappuccino, I would often stop there to satisfy my palate. Most times, the barista and manager, a woman named Laura, would greet me with a heartening smile and then prepare an amazing cappuccino.

I almost never drink my coffee from a paper cup, preferring to sit down, even for a quick ten minutes, to sip my cappuccino from a ceramic cup.

Laura's smile is a treasure. It shines with goodness, caring, curiosity, decency, and happiness. Although I never had a lengthy conversation with Laura, her smile is nonetheless a major inspiration for "SmileRise."

One day, she seemed to be taking longer than usual to select a cup for my coffee. When I asked her if everything was okay, she offered a joyful smile and told me she was trying to pick a cup or mug whose design would best match the cappuccino colors and her milk-froth art.

If the world around you is crumbling down, Laura's good-natured smile will make you forget your cares and bring you peace and serenity. My road trips to Shelburne Falls Coffee Roasters were no longer just about the cappuccino. In the brightness of Laura's therapeutic smile, I found a parallel universe free of the noise that so often overwhelms our world.

A great cappuccino is satisfying and invigorating, no doubt, but the goodness in Laura's smile is priceless to me—and everlasting. I recently learned that she and her husband are expecting a baby girl. Their baby girl is blessed to be born into an extraordinary smile, as the world is blessed because Laura's smile will be passed on to future generations.

Emma's smile

In 2019 I was blessed by an exquisitely elegant smile that is also eternally implanted in my memory. It happened at Blue Loon Bakery, off Main Street, in New London, New Hampshire—about a two-hour drive from my home in Vermont.

Once again, an incredible hot drink and savory pastry played second fiddle to a glimpse of Emma's smile; keep in mind that I am absolutely crazy about tea, cappuccino, and a delicious almond croissant, scone, or muffin. To put things in perspective, for those who remember some episodes from the sitcom Friends, just recall the slogan "Joey doesn't share food…"

In that first encounter, I actually spoke quite extensively to Emma, in Blue Loon's cozy setting that is more fitting for a home than a typical cafe.

Her smile, initially somewhat camouflaged by an awareness of shyness, emerged with a subtle beauty, a tender confidence, a revealing intellect and a strong sense of perception, matters typically reserved for the mind.

Emma's smile emanated of decency, goodness, integrity, fairness and a strong sense of justice and distinction between right and wrong, matters typically reserved for the heart.

Over the many months that followed our first meeting, whenever I was in the presence of Emma's smile, I felt grounded and rooted. For a Taurus like me, nothing is as important as that feeling of stability and connection.

Emma's reassuring smile makes the world a better place in which to live and reestablishes a person's faith in humanity. Simply galvanizing, it also inspired a "SmileRise" poem.

Manchester brunette's smile

Sometimes we get to know the people behind those incredible smiles quite well and on a very personal level. Other times, as they intersect our daily routines and habits for years at a time, bestowers of glorious smiles become an essential part of our lives—but in a limited way, and with an unspoken intimacy. On rare occasions, we catch sight of the most memorable smiles of all: ones that, after a single encounter, remain with us for the rest of our days. Such was the case with the Manchester brunette.

Manchester, Vermont, is one of my favorite quaint towns in New England, nestled at the foothills of the highest summit in the Taconics, Mount Equinox, between the Green Mountains and the Taconic Range. The town is traversed primarily by two streets, Depot Street and Main Street.

I have developed a particular routine for visiting Manchester over the years: I get into my iconic, loyal, rusty, gray, two-door, manual 1991 Jeep Cherokee Sport 4x4 and drive exuberantly for the forty-five minutes between my town of West Dover, Vermont, and Manchester. I say "loyal" because my Jeep has so far gotten stolen twice, yet found its way back to me regardless. I've managed to trim the trip from fifty-five minutes to forty-five or less while discovering just about every dirt road shortcut in the process, coming upon beautiful forests and vistas along the way.

The final stretch of the trip is capped by an awe-inspiring valley descent into town on Route 11 West, passing the Appalachian Trail and Long Trail.

Once in Manchester, I park my car on Depot Street and walk about half a mile up to the roundabout intersection of Main and Depot Streets. There stands my biggest prize of all, Northshire Bookstore, with next-door Bonnet & Main Café (previously Spiral Press Café); the combination of amazing cappuccinos, decadent pastries and inspiring books is just heaven.

Once I arrive, my biggest dilemma is whether to get the cappuccino first or to start by scouring the bookshelves for newly written treasures or ordering a pastry. Of course, there's a fourth draw at Northshire: a smile like no other.

I crisscross the aisles of Northshire's ten-thousand-square-foot mansion of ideas, thoughts, words and pages. Its books are creatively and semi- randomly laid out in the homey environment, and I am in search of that interesting title I've never come across before.

Every once in a while, I look up, only to notice others equally engrossed in very similar missions. In this place, I've come to recognize the meaning behind a certain unsmiling smile:

> *I am here for the serious business of finding a book. I salute you for sharing my interest. I am smiling but I am not smiling, because I have to look serious looking for a book. . . .*

If you open your mind to the possibility, you may spot an amazing unsmiling smile: the understood unforgettable smile.

The Manchester brunette's smile revealed itself not at Northshire Bookstore but nearby, as I made my rounds. Once I have nourished my mind and body at Northshire,

I typically take the Danby marble footpath along Main Street for a brisk one-and-a-half-mile walk to the old village of Manchester Center by Equinox Golf Resort & Spa.

One day, I decided to stop near a store along the path, The Artisan's Key. I had never been inside the store, featuring predominantly women jewelry and accessories made by local artisans. Nevertheless, I had curiously peeked at their windows, as they also carried some beautifully crafted home items and artwork.

As I stood in the parking lot outside the store, I felt the wind and leaves shift as nature rearranged itself to expose a smile beyond compare. Out of nowhere, about forty feet away, a slender, gentle, and elegant brunette was looking straight at me with a smile so familiar I might have known it all my life. It was happy, serene, and respectful, a kind smile representing eternal goodness.

She waved, I waved back, and we just basked in the moment, appreciating it. It was a very long moment indeed. Then she got into her BMW SUV with its New York plates and drove past me wearing that immortal smile, waving goodbye.

A lost moment?

Quite the opposite: a found moment, forever imprinted in my memory. Perchance one day she finds herself reading these words, she may allow for another moment like that in her life.

Collective smile

We think of smiles as belonging to a specific person. There are times, however, when individual smiles combine to radiate a much more powerful and meaningful collective smile.

About six miles south of my town of West Dover, at the intersection of Scenic Route 100 and Route 9, lies the town center of Wilmington, Vermont. Wilmington is a charming small town, with shops, restaurants, galleries, and antique stores housed in enchanting historic buildings. It is only fitting that Wilmington was once home to the American romance novelist Elswyth Thane. Originally from Iowa, Thane is famous for her Williamsburg series comprising seven historical fiction novels (published from 1943 to 1957), including *Dawn's Early Light* (1943).

Wilmington is also home to Bartleby's Books, an amazingly efficient small bookstore, whose owner, Lisa, has an uncanny talent for selecting books that always trigger my interest. As part of my Bartleby's routine, I recently started visiting the newly opened 1a Coffee Roasters. You can easily miss it—the café stands about half a mile west of Route 100, on Route 9 (Main Street) in the direction of Bennington, home of the decisive Revolutionary War Battle of Bennington. If you do miss it, then you will have missed one of the best socially responsible cappuccinos and espressos in New England, not to mention my favorite Finnish korvapuusti cinnamon pastry.

Brian owns and runs 1a with his wife, Chrystal, aided by Aimee. (This is not to understate the importance of their little girls, Addison and Ella.) When I made my first stop at 1a, I did not expect much, but their collective smile, unsuccessfully obscured by masks worn by the adults, immediately captured my heart. Addison and Ella were joyfully playing with their toys in a specially designated carpeted play area, while Brian, an engineering graduate, took meticulous care in assembling a perfectly measured "one-third, one-third, one-third" cappuccino.

Their collective smile—as an establishment, as a family, as a community—is brave, friendly, hopeful, ambitious, caring, and overflowing with goodness. It was a marvelous and uplifting surprise, to say the least. I do not remember the last time I was so touched by the beauty of a collective smile, let alone, a smile that is imbued with youthful aspirations and infinite kindness, unexpectedly suspended on the line-of-ideals between the historical pillars of Bennington and Wilmington.

Heather's smile

Between 2013 and 2017, my son attended Skidmore College in Saratoga Springs, New York. On alternating weekends, just as I would visit my girls at Smith College in Northampton, around seventy miles east of my home in Dover, I would also visit my son at Skidmore, about eighty miles west of Dover. Strictly by coincidence, my home, initially acquired in 1990, turned out to be a virtual midpoint between the two colleges—who knew!

Very often I would stop at beautifully non-renovated South Street Café, in Bennington, Vermont, for an expertly assembled cappuccino and homemade cinnamon roll. For a short while, I was served by a lovely blond woman, whose name I never got to know, but whose smile would fit right in with a Grace Kelly or Audrey Hepburn movie. It radiated poise and elegance, grace and confidence. In the background, open-mic performers sharing their talents gave the patrons yet another reason to smile.

In recent years, the Putnam Block Redevelopment project, an initiative launched to renovate the entire block, caused the café to close its doors. (I hope just temporarily!) That closure led me to experience Heather's smile.

Undaunted in my endless quest for the very best cappuccinos, muffins, pastries, desserts—and, yes, smiles—I scouted Bennington for a new source for all of the above. To my surprise, it was diagonally across the street, at Heather's Bringing You Vermont specialty shop. Unbeknownst to me, at the back of her store was a deli-style café with the best blueberry and triple-berry muffins on the planet. (Granted, I haven't quite traveled the whole world, but my quest has thus far taken me to hundreds of espresso bars, cafés, and bakeries in about thirty countries in the Americas, Europe, and Asia.)

Although the events of 2020–21 have hidden most people's smiles, Heather's is irrepressible. When she smiles, her eyes light up and her cheeks lift. Her smile is tender, dignified, and beautiful. No matter how busy she is or how many deliverables she is multitasking, her happy nature always expresses itself through her smiling face. With a commitment to supporting local artisans, craftspeople, and artists, she projects her smile throughout the community, in a socially responsible and caring manner.

When you behold Heather's smile, you feel the entire community smiling.

Andry's smile

Sometimes my 1991 Jeep Cherokee Sport has a mind of its own.

On the unseasonably warm day of March 12, 2021, as I raced down Mount Snow's Lodge / Upper Exhibition ski slope, the right side of my freshly waxed and sharpened vintage skis—yellow Rossignol Dualtec Race Carvers—got caught in slushy snow. As the left ski completed its slalom hop-and-twist and landed on the right ski, my sliding movement was brought to a sudden halt, hurling my body headfirst down the mountain at high speed, with the right side of my chest taking the brunt of my landing. Initially, I was grateful to have come away unharmed, reattaching my skis and completing my run.

At the bottom of the slope, I decided that perhaps I should take a break by the Main Base Lodge. Inside the lodge, at the Vermont Country Deli's satellite kiosk, was another opportunity to enjoy a cappuccino and the best macaroni and cheese in the Northeast (and possibly the world). During the nonwinter months, I would have had to drive twenty-two miles east of West Dover to the deli's main location on Route 9 in Brattleboro, cutting through the tree-foliage-tunnel of Augur Hole, a dirt road that links Route 100 and Route 9. (I have happily made this trip dozens of times, not only for the mac-and-cheese but also for a truly heavenly almond tart.)

As I lounged on the Adirondack chair outside the lodge, relaxing in the sunshine and reveling in the epicurean bliss of my prized mac-and-cheese, I felt a pain in my chest. My fall was not so harmless as I had thought. Two broken ribs later, I was out of commission for the rest of the ski season.

Not to worry, as this merely meant more weekend road trips for cappuccinos, desserts, and books (following an absolutely fabulous ski season). At this stage, smiles had become almost invisible because of the pandemic. For the rest of the spring, I would get into my Jeep most weekends and drive in the direction of Northshire Bookstore (passing idyllic Jamaica State Park, home of majestic Hamilton Falls).

As I reached the intersection of Route 30 South and Route 11, six miles east of Manchester, my Jeep would decide to veer right on multiple occasions, prompting me to take Route 11 West, away from Manchester. I'd oblige my Jeep's desire, driving past Bromley Mountain and its ski resort and heading four miles westward to Peru, Vermont.

Peru is an unassuming and picturesque town of less than two hundred households. Its downtown on Main Street comprises three notable establishments: J. J. Hapgood General Store, a lovely shack-sized post office, and a community craft workshop and art gallery called Main Street Makery.

Whenever I walk or drive past Suzanne Ragone's Makery to reach J. J. Hapgood, my heart smiles in response to the happiness Suzanne's art, crafts, and workshops have brought so many children and adults alike. The mood set, I proceed to Hapgood, keen on savoring its cappuccino and one of the best moist carrot cakes in the Northeast.

Andry, an enthusiastic young barista wastes no time as he welcomes me and takes my order. The masks of 2020–21 can't obscure his indisputable smile. It beams right through the veil, along with his kindness, humor, and courtesy. As a middle-aged man, I feel energized by the memories Andry calls up in me and the boundless vitality of youth. He proudly takes ownership of his responsibilities and executes them with flawless intent.

The distinctiveness of Andry's smile complements the general store's unique gourmet and merchandise offerings. In addition to the kitchen's creations, you are surrounded by an unexpected and thoughtful selection of items, many featuring words of wisdom and old sayings. They are presented in a historic, warm, old-world-charm milieu, as if to deliberately bring a smile to your heart. To sum it up, it is a delightfully contrasting mélange of old, new, historic and avant-garde, applicable to setting, merchandise and food.

Finally, with the "appetizer mood" set by the Makery, and the "entrée mood" set by the smiling atmosphere of J. J. Hapgood, I continue to the yard for the "dessert mood" of Peru's peacefulness. In March and April, when temperatures would drop below 20 degrees Fahrenheit, I would nevertheless stand at the high table on the outdoor patio, bundled up and slowly sipping my cappuccino while enjoying my carrot cake. I would joyfully take in the scenery, breathing Peru's refreshing air and tapping my foot in time with the classic tunes of Dire Straits coming from Hapgood's outdoor speakers.

As it turns out, my Jeep does not have a mind of its own. The front right brake caliper had malfunctioned, getting stuck in a somewhat engaged position, causing the car to veer slightly right; perhaps my Jeep arranged such a malfunction all those months in order to continually veer us toward the serenity and smiles of Peru.

The thread of time certainly got tangled by the howls of circumstance, highlighted by broken ribs, pandemic, work disruption, seclusion, an interrupted ski season, and more. Nevertheless, ultimately all the knots got untangled and what took precedence to survive in my mind on the thread of time is the related collection of smiles.

So many other smiles likewise inspired "SmileRise": the incredible smile and laughter of my childhood friend of about forty-five years, Lilian; the beautiful and brave-hearted smile of my friend Rama; the respectful and genuine smile of my colleague and friend Michael; the tenderly cautious and radiant smile of Jennifer; the ever-so-loyal smile of my friend and colleague Michael Z.; the sweet smile of Lori; the confidently striking smile of Renee; the reassuring smile of my friend Bassel; the ever-so-glorious smile of Heather, whom I met in Wilmington, at Dot's of Vermont (home of the unexpectedly delicious, seasonal, blueberry sauce swordfish); the perennially optimistic smile of Donna; the unexpectedly endearing smiles of some perfect-stranger baristas—and more. Perhaps those stories will be included in the prologues to future editions of "SmileRise."

Again, life is a collection of smiles threaded by time. This philosophy is a choice. It is my choice. When I choose to anchor life through the endearing moments of a smile, it becomes inevitable that SmileRise poem would manifest itself.

SmileRise Poem

Line-by-Line Visual Presentation

will strangers

once again reveal

<u>unwitting smiles,</u>

to invigorate

my energy,

my mind and my soul

One-hundred-mile

drive,

not for the

cappuccino,

but for the glimpse of

that smile

So easy to bestow,

so hard to get,

so rare to captivate

For the mystery,

the goodness,

the serenity, the

intoxication of that

moment

The flutter

of the heart

and the madness of a

momentary rebirth

One year

has already gone by

A Smile,

Once taken for granted,

Nowhere to be found

Only six feet away, but

sheltering unrevealingly

behind a shy mask

I wonder,

is it curving up

with excitement

at my demi-sight

Or is it disappointedly

cupping down for daring

to pass by

Perhaps

helplessly flatlining,

a permanent feature

for eternity to come

A shot in the arm,

a longing

for a forgotten

SmileRise

hopefully to follow

But not before

an ache is felt,

for every lost smile

that was replaced

by sorrow

Yerini kedere bırakan her kayıp gülümseme için bir acı hissedilir.

A small price to pay,

for the rare precious

curves of tomorrow

That will once again

arouse my spirit

that was once

rendered hollow

Anticipation,

joy,

mystery,

soon the revelation of

smiles no longer

in the shadow.

SmileRise Poem

Verse-by-Verse
Visual Presentation

Will strangers once again reveal unwitting smiles, to invigorate my energy, my mind and my soul

One-hundred-mile drive, not for the Cappuccino, but for the glimpse of that smile

So easy to bestow, so hard to receive, so rare to captivate

For the mystery, the goodness, the serenity, the intoxication of that moment

The flutter of the heart and the madness of a momentary rebirth

❦   ❦   ❦

One year has already gone by

A Smile, once taken for granted, nowhere to be found

Only Six feet away, but sheltering unrevealingly behind a shy mask

I wonder, is it curving up with excitement at my demi-sight

Or is it disappointedly cupping down for daring to pass by

Perhaps helplessly flatlining, a permanent feature for eternity to come

A shot in the arm, a longing for a forgotten SmileRise hopefully to follow

But not before an ache is felt, for every lost smile that was replaced by sorrow

A small price to pay, for the rare precious curves of tomorrow

That will once again arouse my spirit that was once rendered hollow

Anticipation, joy, mystery, soon the revelation of smiles no longer in the shadow.

Thanks

In the following few pages, I want to express thanks to smiles (people), cappuccinos & places and natural settings that inspired SmileRise.

People, places and entities listed in this book have received mention for being part of my story and an integral part of my life (some for many decades). None of them have provided sponsorship nor payment to appear in this book.

Smiles

(In order of book appearance)

Lilian (book dedication)
Laura
Emma
Manchester Brunette
Northshire Bookstore Patrons
Lisa
Brian
Chrystal
Addison
Ella
Aimee
Heather
Andry
Suzanne
Rama
Michael
Jennifer
Michael Z.
Lori
Renee
Bassel
Heather
Donna
State Street Café Blonde
Perfect Stranger Baristas
and more...

Natural Settings

Vermont Green Mountains
(Vermont)

Danby/Dorset Marble Footpath
(Manchester, Vermont)

Mount Equinox
(Manchester, Vermont)

Valley Trail
(Dover, Vermont)

Jamaica State Park
(Jamaica, Vermont)

Hamilton Falls
(Jamaica, Vermont)

Mount Snow
(West Dover, Vermont)

Appalachian Trail/ Long Trail /Bromley Mountain Trail
(Manchester, Vermont)

People, places and entities listed in this book have received mention for being part of my story and an integral part of my life (some for many decades). None of them have provided sponsorship nor payment to appear in this book.

Cappuccinos & Places

Shelburne Falls Coffee Roasters
Shelburne Falls, Northampton & Greenfield Massachusetts

Blue Loon Bakery
New London, New Hampshire

Northshire Bookstore
Manchester, Vermont

Bonnet & Main Café (previously Spiral Press Café)
Manchester, Vermont

The Artisan's Key
Manchester, Vermont

Bartleby's Books
Manchester, Vermont

Coffee 1A Coffee Roasters
Wilmington, Vermont

State Street Café
Bennington, Vermont

Bringing You Vermont
Bennington, Vermont

Vermont Country Deli
Brattleboro & Mount Snow, Vermont

J. J. Hapgood
Peru, Vermont

Main Street Makery
Wilmington, Vermont

Dot's of Vermont
Wilmington, Vermont

People, places and entities listed in this book have received mention for being part of my story and an integral part of my life (some for many decades). None of them have provided sponsorship nor payment to appear in this book.

Index

1943 - 8
1957 - 8
1990 - 9
1991 - 5, 11
1a - 9
1a coffee roasters - 8
2013 - 2, 9
2017 - 9
2019 - 2, 3
2020 - 1, 11, 13
2021 - 1, 11, 13
4x4 - 5

absence - 2
absolutely - 12
accessories - 7
ache - 30, 38
acquired - 9
Addison - 9, 42
Adirondack - 12
adults - 9, 13
affects - 2
aficionado - 2
Aimee - 9, 42
air -14
aisles - 6
allow - 7
almond - 4, 12
alternating - 9
amazing - 2, 6, 8
ambitious - 9
American - 8
Americas - 10
anchor - 15
Andry - 13, 42
Andry's smile - 11
anticipation - 33, 38
antique - 8
Appalachian Trail - 5, 43
appear - 41, 43, 44
appearance - 42
appetizer -14
appreciating - 7
area - 9
arm - 29, 38
arouse - 32, 38
arranged -14
art -13
Artisan's Key - 7, 44
artisans - 7, 11

artists - 11
artwork - 7
Asia - 10
aspirations - 9
assembled - 10
assembling - 9
atmosphere -14
Audrey Hepburn - 10
Augur Hole - 12
avant-garde -14
awareness - 4
away - 25, 37
awe-inspiring - 5

baby - 3
background - 10
bakeries - 10
bakery - 3
barista - 2, 13, 15, 42
barrier - 1
bars - 10
Bartleby's - 8
Bartleby's books - 8, 44
base - 11
basked - 7
Bassel - 15, 42
Battle of Bennington - 8
beams -13
beautiful - 5, 11, 15
beautifully - 7, 10
beauty - 4, 9
behold - 11
belonging - 8
beneath - 25, 37
Bennington - 8, 9, 10, 44
best - 10
bestow - 20, 36
bestowers - 5
blessed - 3
bliss - 12
block - 10
blond - 10
blonde - 42
blue - 3, 4
Blue Loon – 4
Blue Loon Bakery - 3, 44
blueberry - 10, 15
BMW - 7
body - 6, 11, 18, 36
Bonnet & Main Café - 6

book - 2, 6, 8, 12, 41, 42, 43, 44
bookshelves - 6
bookstore - 6, 8
born - 3
bottom - 11
boundless -13
brake -14
Brattleboro - 12, 44
brave - 9
brave-hearted - 15
break - 11
breathing -14
Brian - 9, 42
brightness - 3
Bringing You Vermont - 10, 44
brisk - 7
broken - 12, 14
broken -14
Bromley Mountain - 12
Bromley Mountain Trail - 43
brunette - 4, 5, 6, 7, 42
brunt - 11
buildings - 8
bundled -14
business - 6

café - 4, 8, 10
cake -13, 14
caliper -14
camouflaged - 4
capped - 5
cappuccino - 2, 3, 4, 6, 8, 9, 10, 12, 13, 14, 19, 36, 41, 44
captivate - 20, 36
captured - 9
captures - 2
car - 5, 14
care - 3, 9
caring - 2, 9, 11
carpeted - 9
carrot -13, 14
carvers - 11
catch - 5
caught - 11
cautious - 15
center - 8
ceramic - 2
certainly -14
chair - 12
challenges - 1
charm -14

charming - 8
cheeks - 11
cheese - 12

Cherokee - 11
chest - 11, 12
childhood - 15
children -13
choice - 1, 15
choose - 15
Chrystal - 9, 42
cinnamon - 8, 10
circumstance - 1, 14
classic -14
close - 10
closure - 10
coffee - 2, 3, 8
Coffee 1a Coffee Roasters - 44
coincidence - 9
colleague - 15
collection - 1, 15
collective - 8, 9
college - 2, 9
colors - 3
combination - 6
combine - 8
come - 28, 37
commission - 12
commitment - 11
community - 9, 11, 13
complements -13

completed - 11
completing - 11
complexity
comprises -13
confidence - 4, 10
confidently - 15
connection - 4
continually -14
contrasting -14
conversation - 2
countries - 10
country - 12
courtesy -13
cozy - 4
craft -13
crafted - 7
craftspeople - 11
crazy - 3
creations -13

creatively - 6
crisscross - 6
croissant - 4
crumbling - 3
cup - 2, 3
cupping - 27, 37
curiosity - 2
curving - 26, 37
cutting - 12

daily - 4
Danby - 7, 43
daring - 27, 37
daughters - 2
Dawn's Early Light - 8
day - 3, 5, 7, 11
decadent - 6
decades - 41, 43, 44
decency - 2, 4
decide - 12
decided - 11
decisive - 8
dedication - 42
degrees -14
deli - 12
deliberately -14
delicious - 4, 15
delightfully -14
deli-style - 10
demi-sight - 26, 37
Depot Street - 5
descent - 5
design - 3
designated - 9
desire - 12
dessert - 10, 12, 14
diagonally - 10
difficult - 1
dignified - 11
dilemma - 6
diligence - 1
Dire Straits -14
direction - 8, 12
dirt - 5, 12
disability - 1
disappointedly - 27, 37
discovering - 5
disruption -14
distinction - 4
distinctiveness -13

Donna - 15, 42
doors - 10
Dorset marble footpath - 43
Dot's of Vermont - 15, 44
doubt - 3
dove - 7
Dover - 9, 43
down - 11, 27, 37
downtown -13
dozens - 12
draw - 6
drink - 2, 3
drive - 3, 12, 13, 19, 36
driving - 12
Dualtec - 11

east - 9, 12
easy - 20, 36
editions - 2, 15
efficient - 8
eighty - 9
elegance - 10
elegant - 3, 7
Ella - 9, 42
Elswyth Thane - 8
emanated - 4
emerged - 4
Emma - 3, 4, 42
Emma's smile - 3
emotion - 1
enchanting - 8
encounter - 1, 4, 5
endearing - 15
endless - 10
energized -13
engaged -14
engineering - 9
engrossed - 6
enjoy - 12
enjoying -14
enthusiastic -13
entities - 41, 43, 44
entrée -14
environment - 6
epicurean - 12
episodes - 4
Equinox Golf Resort & Spa - 7
era - 1
espresso - 8, 10
essential - 5

establishment - 9, 13
eternal - 7
eternally - 3
eternity - 28, 37
Europe - 10
eventual - 2
everlasting - 1, 3
evoked - 2
excitement - 26, 37
executes -13
expecting - 3
experience - 10
expertly - 10
expose - 7
express - 41
expresses - 11
exquisitely - 3
extensively - 4
extraordinary - 2, 3
exuberantly - 5
eyes - 11

fabulous - 12
face - 11
Fahrenheit -14
fairness - 4
faith - 4
fall - 12
familiar - 2, 7
family - 9
famous - 8
favorite - 5, 8
featuring -13
feeling - 2, 4
feet - 7, 25, 37
felt - 30, 38
fiction - 8
fiddle - 3
fifty-five - 5
final - 5
finding - 6
finnish - 8
first - 4
fitting - 4, 8
flatlining - 28, 37
flawless -13
flutter - 22, 36
foliage - 12
follow - 29, 38
following - 41

food - 4, 14
foothills - 5
footpath - 7, 43
forests - 5
forget - 3
forgotten - 29, 38
forty - 7
forty-five - 5,15
found - 24, 37
four -13
free - 3
freshly - 11
friend - 4, 15
friendly - 9
front -14
future - 2, 3, 15

galleries - 8
gallery -13
galvanizing - 4
general -13
general store -13
generations - 3
gentle - 7
genuine - 15
get - 20, 36
girl - 3, 9
glimpse - 3, 19, 36
glorious - 5, 15
gone - 23, 37
goodbye - 7
good-natured - 3
goodness - 1, 2, 3, 4, 7, 9, 21, 36
gourmet -13
grace - 10
Grace Kelly - 10
graduate - 9
granted - 10, 24, 37
grateful - 11
gray - 5
great - 3
Green Mountains - 5, 43
Greenfield - 44
greet - 2
grounded - 4

habits - 5
half - 5, 8
halt - 11
Hamilton Falls - 12, 43

Hapgood -13, 14
happily - 12
happiness - 2, 13
happy - 7, 11
hard - 20, 36
harmless - 12
headfirst - 11
heading -13
heart - 4, 9, 13, 14, 22, 36
heartening - 2
Heather - 9, 10, 11, 15, 42
Heather's smile - 9
heaven - 6
heavenly - 12
helplessly - 28, 37
hidden - 11
high - 11
highest - 5
highlighted -14
historic - 8, 13, 14
historical - 8, 9
hollow - 32, 38
home - 2, 3, 4, 7 8, 9, 12, 15
homemade - 10
homey - 6
hop-and-twist - 11
hopeful - 9
hopefully - 29, 38
hot - 3
housed - 8
households -13
howl - 1, 14
humanity - 4
humor -13
hundred - 10, 13, 19, 36
hurling - 11
husband - 3

iconic - 5
ideals - 9
ideas - 6
idyllic - 12
imbued - 9
immediately - 9
immortal - 7
implanted - 3
impressions - 1
imprinted - 7
included - 15
incredible - 3, 4, 15

indisputable -13
individual - 8
inevitable - 15
infinite - 9
initially - 4, 11
initiative - 10
inspiration - 2
inspired - 4, 15, 41
inspiring - 6
integral - 41, 43, 44
integrity - 1, 4
intellect - 4
intent -13
interest - 6, 8
interesting - 6
interrupted -14
intersect - 4
intersection - 5, 8, 12
intimacy - 5
intoxication - 21, 36
invigorate - 18, 36
invigorating - 3
invisible - 12
Iowa - 8
irrepressible - 11
items - 7
J. J. Hapgood - 13, 14, 44
Jamaica - 43
Jamaica state park - 12, 43
Jeep - 5, 12, 14
Jeep cherokee sport - 5, 11
Jennifer - 15, 42
jewelry - 7
Joey - 4
joy - 33, 38
joyful - 3
joyfully - 9, 14
justice - 4
keen -13
kind - 7
kindness - 9, 13
kiosk - 12
kitchen -13
knew - 10
knots - 1, 14
know - 10
korvapuusti - 8
landed - 11
landing - 11
laughter - 15

Index | 51

launched - 10
Laura - 2, 3, 42
leaves - 7
left - 11
level - 4
life - 1, 7, 15, 41, 43, 44
lift - 11
light - 11
Lilian - 15, 42
limited - 5
line-by-line - 17
line-of-ideals - 9
links - 12
Lisa - 8, 42
listed - 41, 43, 44
lives - 5
local - 7, 11
location - 12
lodge - 11, 12
logistics - 1
long - 7
Long Trail - 5, 43
longing - 29, 38
Loon - 3, 4
Lori - 15, 42
loss - 1
lost - 7, 30, 38
lot - 7
lounged - 12
lovely - 10, 13
loyal - 5, 15
MA-2 - 2
mac-and-cheese - 12
macaroni - 12
madness - 22, 36
main - 3, 5, 12
Main Base Lodge - 11
Main Street - 3, 5, 7, 8, 13
Main Street Makery - 13, 44
majestic - 12
Makery -13, 14
malfunction -14
malfunctioned -14
man -13
manager - 1, 2
Manchester - 4, 5, 6, 12, 42, 43, 44
Manchester brunette - 4, 5
Manchester center - 7
manifest - 15
manner - 11

mansion - 6
manual - 5
marble - 7, 43
marvelous - 9
mask - 9, 13, 25, 37
Massachusetts - 2, 44
match - 3
meaning - 6
meaningful - 8
measured - 9
meeting - 4
mélange -14
memorable - 5
memories -13
memory - 3, 7
mention - 41, 43, 44
merchandise -13, 14
meticulous - 9
Michael - 15, 42
Michael Z. - 15, 42
middle-aged -13
midpoint - 10
mile - 5, 8, 9, 12, 13, 19, 36
milieu -14
milk-froth-art - 3
mind - 3, 4, 6, 11, 14, 15, 18, 36
minutes - 2, 5
missions - 6
Mohawk Trail - 2
moist -13
moment - 7, 15, 21, 36
momentary - 22, 36
months - 4, 12, 14
mood -13, 14
Mount Equinox - 5, 43
Mount Snow - 11, 43, 44
mountain - 11, 12
movement - 11
movie - 10
muffin - 4, 10
mug - 3
multiple - 12
multitasking - 11
mystery - 21, 36, 33, 38
name - 10
natural - 41
natural settings - 43
nature - 7, 11
nestled - 5
new -14

New England - 5, 8
New Hampshire - 3, 44
New London - 3, 44
New York - 7, 9
newly - 8
next-door - 6
noise - 3
non-renovated - 10
nonwinter - 12
Northampton - 2, 9, 44
Northeast - 12, 13
Northshire - 6
Northshire Bookstore - 6, 12, 42, 44
notable -13
nourished - 6
novelist - 8
novels - 8
nowhere - 24, 37

oblige - 12
obscure -13
obscured - 9
occasions - 5, 12
offerings -13
office -13
old - 7, 13, 14
one - 19, 36
one-and-a-half-mile - 7
one-third - 9
open - 6
opened - 8
open-mic - 10
opportunity - 12
opposite - 7
optimistic - 15
order - 13, 42
outdoor -14
overflowing - 9
overwhelms - 3
owner - 8
ownership -13

pages - 6, 41
pain - 12
palate - 2
pandemic - 12, 14
paper - 2
parallel - 3
park - 5, 12
parking - 7

part - 41, 43, 44
pass - 27, 37
passing - 5, 12
pastries - 6, 10
pastry - 3, 6, 8
path - 7
patience - 1
patio -14
patrons - 10, 42
pay - 31, 38
payment - 41, 43, 44
peace - 3
peacefulness -14
peeked - 7
people - 2, 4, 11, 41, 43, 44
perception - 4
perchance - 7
perennially - 15
perfect - 15, 42
perfectly - 9
performers - 10
perhaps - 28, 37
person - 8
personal - 2, 4
perspective - 4
Peru - 13, 14, 44
philosophy - 1, 15
picturesque -13
pillars - 9
place - 4, 41, 43, 44
planet - 10
plates - 7
play - 9
playing - 9
poem - 2, 4, 15, 17, 35
poise - 10
position -14
possibility - 6
post -13
powerful - 8
precedence -14
precious - 31, 38
prepare - 2
presence - 4
presentation - 17, 35
presented -13
price - 31, 38
priceless - 3
prize - 6
prized - 12

proceed -13
process - 5
project - 10, 11
prologue - 1, 2, 15
prompting - 12
published - 8
Putnam Block Redevelopment - 10

quaint - 5
quest - 10

Race Carvers - 11
raced - 11
radiant - 15
radiate - 8
radiated - 10
Ragone -13
Rama - 15, 42
rare - 5, 20, 31, 36, 38
rearranged - 7
reason - 10
reassuring - 4, 15
reattaching - 11
rebirth - 22, 36
received - 41, 43, 44
recent - 10
recognize - 6
redevelopment - 10
reflects - 2
refreshing -14
related - 15
relaxing - 12
remember - 9
rendered - 32, 38
Renee - 15, 42
renovate - 10
replaced - 30, 38
reserved - 4
resort -13
respectful - 7, 15
response -13
responsibilities -13
responsible - 8, 11
restaurants - 8
return - 2
reveal - 18, 36
revealed - 6
revealing - 4
revelation - 33, 38
reveling - 12

Revolutionary War - 8
ribs - 12, 14
right -11, 12, 14
road - 2, 3, 5, 12
roasters - 2, 3, 8
roll - 10
romance - 8
rooted - 4
Rossignol Dualtec Race Carvers - 11
roundabout - 5
rounds - 6
Route 100 - 8, 12
Route 11 - 5, 12
Route 30 - 2
Route 9 - 8, 12
routine - 4, 5, 8
run - 11
rusty - 5

salute - 6
Saratoga Springs - 9
satellite - 12
satisfy - 2
satisfying - 3
sauce - 15
savoring -13
savory - 3
sayings -13
scarcity - 1
scenery -14
scenic - 8
scone - 4
scouring - 6
scouted - 10
season - 12, 14
seasonal - 15
seclusion -14
second - 3
security - 4
selecting - 8
semi-randomly - 6
sense - 4
serene - 7
serenity - 3, 14, 21, 36
series - 8
serious - 6
setting - 4, 14, 41
seven - 8
seventy - 9
shack-sized -13

shadow - 33, 38
sharpened - 11
Shelburne Falls - 2, 3, 44
Shelburne Falls Coffee Roasters - 44
sheltering - 25, 37
shift - 7
shines - 2
shop - 8, 10
short - 2
short-lived - 1
shot - 29, 38
shy - 25, 37
shyness - 4
side - 11
sight - 1, 5, 26, 37
similar - 6
single - 5
sip - 2
sipping -14
sitcom - 4
six - 8, 12, 25, 37
ski -11, 12, 13, 14
Skidmore College - 9
skis - 11
slalom - 11
slender - 7
sliding - 11
slogan - 4
slope - 11
slushy - 11
small - 8, 31, 38
smile - 1, 2, 3, 4, 5, 6, 7, 8, 9, 10, 11, 12, 13, 14, 15, 18, 19, 24, 30, 31, 33, 36, 37, 38, 41, 42
SmileRise - 2, 4, 15, 17, 29, 35, 38, 41
smiling - 6, 11, 14
Smith - 2
Smith College - 9
snow - 11
socially - 8, 11
son - 9
sorrow - 30, 38
soul – 18, 36
source - 10
south - 8, 12
South Street Café - 10
speakers -14
specially - 9, 10
specific - 8
speed - 11
Spiral Press Cafe - 6, 44
spirit - 32, 38

sponsorship - 41, 43, 44
sport - 11
spot - 6
spring - 12
state - 12
State Street Café - 44
State Street Café blonde - 42
stolen - 5
stood - 7
stop - 7, 9, 10
store - 7, 8, 10, 13
stories - 15
story - 41, 43, 44
stranger - 15, 18, 36
stranger baristas - 42
street - 3, 5, 10
strength - 1
stretch - 5
striking - 15
strong - 4
stuck -14
subside - 1
subtle - 4
sudden - 11
summit - 5
sunshine - 12
supporting - 11
surprise - 2, 9, 10
survive -14
suspended - 9
sustained - 2

suv - 7
Suzanne - 13, 42
sweet - 15
swordfish - 15

table -14
Taconic Range - 5
Taconics - 5
taken - 24, 37
talent - 8, 10
tangled - 1, 14
tapping -14
tart - 12
Taurus - 4
tea - 3
temperatures -14
temporarily - 10
temporary - 1
tender - 4

tender - 4, 11
tenderly - 15
ten-thousand-square-foot - 6
Thane - 8
thankful - 2
thanks - 41
The Artisan's Key - 7
therapeutic - 3
thirty - 10
thought - 6, 12
thoughtful -13
thread - 1, 14, 15
threaded - 1, 15
three -13
time - 1, 2, 4, 5, 9, 12, 13, 14, 15
title - 6
tomorrow - 31, 38
touched - 9
town - 5, 8, 13
toys - 9
traveled - 10
traversed - 5
treasure - 2, 6
tree-foliage-tunnel - 12
trigger - 8
trip - 2, 3, 5, 12
triple-berry - 10
true - 1
tunes -14
tunnel - 12
turned - 10
twenty-two - 12
twice - 5
two-door - 5
two-hour - 3
typical - 4

unassuming -13
unavailability - 1
unbeknownst - 10
uncanny - 8
undaunted - 10
understood - 6
unexpected -13
unexpectedly - 9, 15
unforgettable - 2, 6
unharmed - 11
unique -13
universe - 3
unravel - 1

unrevealingly - 25, 37
unseasonably - 11
unsmiling - 6
unspoken - 5
unsuccessfully - 9
untangled -14
unwitting - 18, 36
uplifting - 9
Upper Exhibition - 11

valley - 5
Valley Trail - 43
veer - 12, 14
veil -13
Vermont - 2, 3, 5, 8, 10, 13, 43, 44
Vermont Country Deli - 12, 44
Vermont Green Mountains - 43
verse-by-verse - 35
village - 7
vintage - 11
virtual - 10
visit - 9
visiting - 5
vistas - 5
visual - 17, 35
vitality -13

walk - 5, 7, 13
want - 41
war - 8
warm - 11, 13
wastes -13
waved - 7
waving - 7
waxed - 11
way - 5
wearing - 7
weekend - 9, 12
welcomes -13
west - 5, 8, 9, 12
West Dover - 5, 8, 12, 43
westward -13
wife - 9
Williamsburg - 8
Wilmington - 8, 9, 15, 44
wind - 1, 7
windows - 7
wisdom -13
woman - 2, 7, 10
wonder - 1, 26, 37

words - 6, 7, 13
work - 1, 14
workshop -13
world - 3, 4, 10, 12
world-charm -14
worn - 9
worry - 12
written - 6
wrong - 4
yard -14
year - 1, 5, 10, 15, 23, 37
yellow - 11
young -13
youth -13
youthful - 9

CPSIA information can be obtained
at www.ICGtesting.com
Printed in the USA
BVHW041942240721
612615BV00007B/187/J